FRAGMENTS IN A CLOSET

DAISY ODEY

Published by Akashic Books
©2019 Daisy Odey

ISBN: 978-1-61775-747-1

Akashic Books
Brooklyn, New York, USA
Ballydehob, Co. Cork, Ireland
Twitter: @AkashicBooks
Facebook: AkashicBooks
E-mail: info@akashicbooks.com
Website: www.akashicbooks.com

African Poetry Book Fund
Prairie Schooner
University of Nebraska
110 Andrews Hall
Lincoln, Nebraska 68588

TABLE OF CONTENTS

In "Naming," the opening poem from Daisy Odey's chapbook *Fragments in a Closet*, the narrator begins with an invocation:

> I call the water over my head roof.
> Now the river is home,
> And drowning is an art of living.
> A girl opens her mouth . . .
> I walk tongue first into myself.

Here, in "Naming," we have the literal *naming*. Through this act, the narrator reclaims language: "call," "mouth," "tongue"; reclaims action: "call," "is," "drowning," "opens," "walk"; and thus reclaims selfhood—expressed through the aforesaid voice, action, and choice of meaning—making to define the self. Here is the taking of agency and the birthing of self, foreshadowing the feminist construct she will later further illuminate, such as in the poem aptly titled "Feminist:" "I was my mother's daughter before I wore my father's name. She put her / voice in my body."

This introductory invocation and purposed announcement of what is to come has long been a familiar trope of poetry. Here, in Odey's capable hands, we have the allusion to the song of the West African griot, the custodian of culture and song. The griot is more than the "holder of story" as we understand it in the West—the griot holds the stories of the culture, the people, the family lineages, the community, as well as the fictional narratives, parables, and poems. Reflecting this tradition, for Odey, the poem becomes a calling, a haunting, an announcing—an invocation to the ancestors, to the community, to the orisha Oshun, to the creation of self.

In "Naming," the allusion to Oshun—Yoruba orisha of birth/rebirth, purity, fertility, love, and sensuality, who is always identified with water, specifically rivers—sets the stage for a developing and unifying motif in the chapbook. Water saturates Odey's text; water is in titles—"How to Make A River," "Life Is Water," "Falling for a River"—water is in the theme, subject matter, character, and narrative development, and, of course, in the imagery—powerful, inventive, haunting: "if we call out over the water and it replies in a familiar voice from our chil- / dren's throat, we know our fathers died by drowning" ("Origins").

In the poem "How to Make a River," Odey extends the imagery of her exploration of water to the role of other aspects of the natural world:

> Pull my mother's eyes
> from my sockets
> Make the sun and a moon.

It is fitting that it is not just water, with all its rich allusions in Nigerian cultures, that is explored in this poetry collection, but also the sun, the earth, fire, storms, etc. These concerns about an identification and personhood of such aspects of nature are strongly present in the work of contemporary African poets.

It is refreshingly exciting to see how a skilled African poet like Daisy Odey privileges a black intellectual and creative construct and black mythos in the real or natural world. This specific way of balancing between the literal and figurative—which is how a certain type of African consciousness engages with being, and thus with language in both the real and the imagined—has become one of the most exciting things about the continent's contemporary poetry and the recent, contemporary black diaspora. In Odey's hands, the language is lush, the imagery virtuosic.

Consider "Tourist": "you hold the sun in your mouth, / and tell me the taste of light . . ." And, in "How to Make A River," she writes:

> When asked to show love

I blend the honey brown of your skin
with the salt of my sweat
make a river.

Like many contemporary African writers, the specter of colonialism, as
well as those of postcolonial conflicts (in this case the Nigerian-Biafra Civil
War) makes an appearances in the text. "'Is there a god worthy of war?'"
the speaker of "Fragments" asks. In "Peace Maker," the narrator reflects:
"through the eye of a gun every man is a country and belief is constitution."
And in "Broke," the speaker reflects on the fact that "there is a torn continent / between these thighs."

But Odey's deft handling of the specter of war is graceful; violence
haunts the text as seen from the corner of the eye, but is not the subject
of the text. The subject is rebirth, reclaiming, foregrounding. How do we
create ourselves as contemporary African women outside of the forces that
have shaped our country and our being? For there is a separate, specific
experience of war that women endure that is distinct from the experience
of men.

Thus, these themes of spirituality, selfhood, and violence that perme-
ate the text surround the idea of gender, a key aspect of this collection. In
"Feminist," which, like "Naming," is grounded in Nigerian themes of gender and spirituality—Oshun again—the narrator recounts, "when I asked my
mother, *How do I wear woman?*' she replied, *How does water wear wet?*'"

Odey interrogates the nature of the body, exploring its many meanings,
functions, and forms. In "Birthmark," Odey writes:

You do not know this yet
as you do not know that big men
in little girl's bodies grow,
become strangers in themselves.

Observable in the work of American contemporary diasporic writers of color—like Safia Sinclair, Solmaz Sharif, Ocean Voung, and Safyia Elhillo—is an interrogration of the diasporic relationship to culture and language that has been thrust upon their bodies and minds through white violence, colonization, and exploitation, and theft, creating a space where this interrogation of language, particularly the violence of English, has itself become a contemporary, mythic trope.

In "How to Make A River," Odey's narrator states: "I bring all of myself / I show all that is woman in me." Here, we return to the figure of Oshun to embody themes of identity, (re)creation, and agency. Despite history, despite violence, the hero of Odey's narrative is not frozen in trauma, fragmented. The hero, the narrator, is brought to Oshun, this embodiment of creation, this magnificently powerful force, this joy and beauty of the immortal divinity of black womanhood that can never be destroyed by the violence of colonization, and other violences and fractures. "How do we drown a river?" Odey asks in "Fragments"—and thus, the hero is created anew.

NAMING

I call the water over my head roof.
Now the river is home,
And drowning is an art of living.
A girl opens her mouth . . .
I walk tongue first into myself.

I call her love, and pretend she will stay.
I call my mother life, now she will live forever.
I call my father water.
I call myself wind.
Even as he leaves,
he remains the fluid part of me.

ORIGIN

If we call out over the water and it replies in a familiar voice from our children's throat, we know our fathers died by drowning. This is reincarnation. The ocean always responds. The bed of the Atlantic is an African cemetery; there is a lost continent there.

At birth my father named me Osun, a place. As I roam the world I never leave home. My mother named me Oshun, a god. As I pray I hear my voice call out to me to save myself.

A distant aunt says I am like my father, a well, a thing that's always hungry. I think I am like my mother, a wanderer.

Together these two things can only birth a river, water that never stops running. The shore is a woman; she doesn't taste my father in our first kiss. Soon our clothes are on the floor, and I think how half in itself is still whole.

FRAGMENTS

Yesterday
we fought fire with water.
Today
a flood is killing our children.
How do we drown a river?

Tongues tied with grief forget the language of prayer.
Heavy hearts do not carry love.
Some questions are always hungry,
like:
"Is there a god worthy of war?"

PEACEMAKER

Let us not strike each other, not even with a leaf of grass. —Ladan Osman

Those who grow through war fight, only for peace.

When the treaties are signed and we dig up the earth, do the buried come
up undead? On the list, if we have the least casualties, does that mean we
win? Wait. Tell that answer to Terver's corpse. Then ask my grandfather if
the light of half of a yellow sun would ever shine as bright as a whole one.

In this city, every ridge has a name, every name is a memory. So when the
wind raises dust, nostalgia hangs in the air. With every breath we *un-forget.*
Death is cold, but war is colder.

Through the eye of a gun, every man is a country and belief is constitution.
What's wrong is we are all right. On paper, death is a story we can still
retell. I write the river of blood back into the corpses, tell myself this is
why we kill: to experience resurrection. Tell myself the world is a sphere,
because at every end we are meant to *re-begin.*

BECAUSE

Because your English teacher warned
"never begin a sentence with because"
and life taught you
your teachers were never right.

Because girls are light
and Jos is a city of light
because you love your mother
you tell her you love Jos.

Because Lagos is a tease
and teases never deliver what they promise
on every street we see
concrete skeletons of big dreams.

Because black is void
and white is light
because voids can be filled
but light is already full of itself.

FEMINIST

I was my mother's daughter before I wore my father's name. She put her voice in my body because when there's a storm in my spirit I'd need a shield in my throat.

This is all I know; that to be born in this body is to be born behind bars and only those who master their prisons are able to break it.

When I asked my mother, "How do I wear woman?" she replied, "How does water wear wet?'"

TOURIST

You hold the sun in your mouth,
and tell me the taste of light . . .

Halima,
you carry gracefully the places you have been between your teeth

Tell me
if we kiss
can I pretend
I'm taking a trip?

LIFE IS WATER

Water is a mirror.
It doesn't need a dark side
to reflect who we are.
Life is water.

The sea is an outstretched arm.
There is nothing it takes
it can keep.
Nothing it keeps
it will not soon forget.
The heart is a sea.

Pleasure is the cousin of deceit,
deceit the bed mate of ignorance,
ignorance is not innocence,
innocence is not fear,
fear is not respect,
respect is not silence.

Silence is death.

HOW TO MAKE A RIVER

When asked to show love
I blend the honey brown of your skin
with the salt of my sweat
make a river.

Pull my mother's eyes
from my sockets
Make the sun and a moon.
I bring all of myself
I show all that is woman in me.

BROKE

No one finds love
looking into broken
bones or wilting flowers.
There is little certainty
of revival
in dying things.

I love you shooting star,
fleeting as you are.
Will you love
a planet in return?

There is a torn continent
between these thighs
praying to become a home.
There is a nation
of children that will love you
with conked out bones
and speak a thousand languages
your body understands

I am a casualty
of good intentions.
This broke heart is full
emptiness is all it has.

There is war in this spirit that has left fragments
you should love wholly.
My palms grow flowers.

Do not be fooled
by their fragrance
they come with thorns.
I love you shooting star,
fleeting as you are.
Will you love
a planet in return?

GENEALOGY

I am my mother's daughter.
I wear her crown—
black locks
hand twisted by fate.

When she died
she said,
"This is when I become god
this is where you become me."

Our home was match wood:
my father fuel,
my mother water.
So it didn't burn.
Mother was pollen,
father, Wind.
He left a piece of her wherever he went.
My mother is everywhere.
I am my father's daughter—
everywhere is home.

My blood is the river
that borders my love.
They taste the words
"you do not build your future
on a thing that's always running
running from itself."

BODY COUNT

If you look too closely, everything breaks your heart. —Ben Okri

We peel old lovers off our bodies,
hold the taste of memory on our tongues,
christen the ceremony
"lovemaking."
Undressed, we become
two crescents to the night of a room.
I fill your body like air.
Together, We become full.

It's morning;
the petals of our fingers
loosen their grip.
We open up to sunlight
I tell you
I want more
than to live for empty spaces.
I am walking away from being an echo.
I tell you
my darkness is home.
It is your light that brought in the shadows.
I am happy alone.

We dress
in solid silence,
add new layers to already thick skin.
You have no words for a body
that only speaks touch.

AFTER THE REQUIEM

A boy smiled at me today,
with mouth full of your teeth.
He whistled my name,
held out your hands,
and I filled them.

Today is a bad day.
My tongue is aflame,
but you are a dam in my throat—
you drown my words.

I cannot say,
"One of us wears a body
they cannot call home."

Home is a black hole
when your universe is gone.
Laughter in grief is cyanide
on the skin of the universe;
one man's darkness
is a little too light.

EQUALITY

Every body is a corpse,
everybody is a soul
in death
genderless
all human
none the less.

FALLING FOR A RIVER

Someone I loved once gave me a box full of darkness. —Mary Oliver

The night is still, the earth has stopped breathing, no evening breeze, no
gentle flutter to tickle the trees, the windows don't clap against the sill.

This heart has stopped beating, I feel around the numb for a pulse.
Something to say "life is here."
But this is not death.

I walk to work and back still, I drink coffee, I dream dreams.
But this is not life.

The head warns the heart, *You cannot love a river it will always kiss different
shores at once.*

MOURNING

In the gut of a river,
I find undigested remains,
where my brother trailed off like a sentence
led towards an uncertain future.

This body holds wood and steel as lover
yet evicts a boy after calling his lungs "home."
Only earth gives life
after feeding on dead things.

There is a stranger in a box
the breadth of a boy's life.
He is blue as the Irises dying between my mother's
fingers.
Now he lies
a part of all he was
yet apart from it.

I pull my brother
from the wetness of my grief.
Put him on a scale, measure,
how light is the dawn of darkness?

SOUL MATES

Hold your head in your hands.
Pretend to rock your body to sleep.
You opened your heart to the wind,
fell in love with a thing that wanders.

Now home is never where you last left it.
Your shadow asks why you keep trying to die.
You say that is the only way you know how to live.

Take photographs of her every chance you get.
Hold pixels of her soul trapped in a moment.
Put them beside yours in a breast pocket,
there you are legally soul mates.

INCOMPLETE

Your sweat on my pillow is drying,
in this room where we first walked in together,
where we last walked into each other.
I fill my nostrils and hold my breath;
This is how I want to keep you,
full within me.
This is also how to die,
to never exhale,
to hold on to another
while we lose ourselves.

BIRTHMARK

Since color is country,
at every new moon
a body speaks a new tongue.
You do not know this yet
as you do not know that big men
in little girl's bodies grow,
become strangers in themselves.

The day is the color of guilt
when you tell a girl you love her.
The day is the color of rain
when you kiss her
before she tells her mother,
before neighbours fold into wallets of prayer
and ask what you seek in their daughters' throats.

"Birthmark," you say.
Love is a birthmark.

Naked
there are two yous.
God stares back from the mirror
"Why?"
You mumble.
All the books in the world
and no answers;
all religions of the world,
and no cure.

But color is country,
and every new moon
your body speaks a new tongue.
You know this now
as you know the many
who are not the flesh they wear
make home in the closets of their shadows.

ACKNOWLEDGMENTS

With grateful acknowledgements to the editors of the following publications where these poems have appeared, some in earlier versions:

Saraba: "Birthmark" (Issue 12),
Kalahari Review: "Reflections," "Fragments"
Praxis Magazine International Women's Day Anthology: "Equality" (2017)
Afridiaspora: "Mourning"
SEVHAGE: "Origin," "Body Count," "Peacemaker"